CELEBRATING THE NAME BARBARA

Celebrating the Name Barbara

Walter the Educator

Silent King Books a WhichHead Imprint

Copyright © 2024 by Walter the Educator

All rights reserved. No part of this book may be reproduced in any manner whatsoever without written permission except in the case of brief quotations embodied in critical articles and reviews.

First Printing, 2024

Disclaimer
This book is a literary work; poems are not about specific persons, locations, situations, and/or circumstances unless mentioned in a historical context. This book is for entertainment and informational purposes only. The author and publisher offer this information without warranties expressed or implied. No matter the grounds, neither the author nor the publisher will be accountable for any losses, injuries, or other damages caused by the reader's use of this book. The use of this book acknowledges an understanding and acceptance of this disclaimer.

dedicated to everyone with the first
name of Barbara

CONTENTS

Dedication v

One - Masterpiece Of Love 1

Two - Barbara's Name 3

Three - Truly Adored 5

Four - Strength And Grace 7

Five - Priceless Emblem 9

Six - Here's To You, Barbara 11

Seven - Name So Divine 13

Eight - Guiding Light 15

Nine - Name Resounds 17

Ten - Promise Of Tomorrow 19

Eleven - Dances In The Morning Light 21

Twelve - Precious And Rare 23

Thirteen - Diamond In The Sky 25

Fourteen - Hope And Love 27

Fifteen - Every Dream 29

Sixteen - Glory 31

Seventeen - Spun Gold 33

Eighteen - Rivers That Flow 35

Nineteen - Echoes Through The Ages 37

Twenty - Every Prayer 39

Twenty-One - Unyielding Power 41

Twenty-Two - Dances In The Air 43

Twenty-Three - Wondrous Space 45

Twenty-Four - Love And Cheer 47

Twenty-Five - Fair And Sweet 49

Twenty-Six - Everlasting Mystery 51

Twenty-Seven - Rare Flower 53

Twenty-Eight - Resonates 55

Twenty-Nine - Treasure To Embrace 57

Thirty - Beyond Any Dream 59

Thirty-One - Illustrious Legacy 61

Thirty-Two - Work Of Art 63

Thirty-Three - Raise A Toast 65

Thirty-Four - Your Name 67

About The Author 69

ONE

MASTERPIECE OF LOVE

Barbara, oh Barbara, your name sings
In the winds, it dances, and it rings
A melody of strength and grace
In every step, in every embrace
In fields of gold and skies of blue
Barbara, your name shines through
A beacon of hope, a guiding light
In the darkest hour, in the blackest night
Oh, Barbara, your name holds power
In every sunrise, in every flower
It weaves a tale of love and might
A symphony of joy, a dance of delight
In every whisper, in every prayer
Barbara, your name fills the air

With kindness, warmth, and endless bliss
A river of dreams, a tender kiss
    So here's to you, Barbara, so true
In every sunset, in every dew
Your name, a treasure, a work of art
A masterpiece of love, a beating heart

TWO

BARBARA'S NAME

Oh Barbara, blessed with grace and charm,
Your name like music, a soothing balm.
In every letter, a story unfolds,
A tale of strength that never grows old.

Beneath the sky so vast and bright,
Barbara shines like a guiding light.
A beacon of hope in the darkest night,
Her name a melody, pure and right.

From the hills to the ocean's shore,
Barbara's name we proudly adore.
A symphony of beauty, a work of art,
Engraved in every beating heart.

In fields of green and meadows fair,
Barbara's name dances in the air.
A whisper of love, a promise true,
In every sunrise, in every dew.

So let us raise our voices high,
And sing of Barbara to the sky.
For in her name, we find our way,
A shining star that will never sway.

Oh Barbara, in your name we find,
A universe of wonder, one of a kind.
So let us cherish and hold it dear,
For Barbara's name, forever sincere.

THREE

TRULY ADORED

Oh, Barbara, bearer of beauty and grace,
In your name, there's a melody, a sweet embrace.
Like a radiant star in the dark night sky,
Your name shines brightly, catching every eye.

Barbara, with each syllable, a symphony of sound,
A name so elegant, so profound.
In the garden of names, yours blooms like a rose,
A timeless classic, a name that proudly shows.

From ancient times to the modern day,
Barbara, your name has found its way,
Through history's pages, it stands tall and true,
A name that's cherished, through and through.

In every letter, a story to be told,
In every sound, a treasure to behold.
Barbara, a name that echoes through the ages,

Carrying wisdom in its syllables, throughout history's pages.

So here's to Barbara, a name of strength and light,
A name that shines through the darkest night.
In every corner of the world, your name is known,
Barbara, a name that stands alone.

May your name be celebrated, cherished, and adored,
For Barbara, you are truly adored.

FOUR

STRENGTH AND GRACE

Barbara, oh name of strength and grace,
A beacon of light in every space.
With each syllable, a symphony of power,
A name that blooms like a rare flower.

In the gardens of language, Barbara stands tall,
A melody of consonants, a rhythm to enthrall.
With each letter, a story untold,
Of courage, wisdom, and hearts of gold.

Barbara, a name that echoes through time,
A legacy of resilience, a reason to climb.
In the tapestry of names, unique and rare,
Barbara shines bright, beyond compare.

From the shores of distant lands,
To the mountains where freedom stands,

Barbara, a name that conquers all,
A warrior's call, never to fall.
 So let us raise our voices high,
And sing the praises of Barbara, nigh.
For in this name, a universe unfurls,
A symphony of strength, for all the world.
 Barbara, oh name of legend and might,
A guiding star in the darkest night.
In every heartbeat, in every breath,
Barbara, a name that conquers death.

FIVE

PRICELESS EMBLEM

Oh, Barbara, your name rings like a bell,
In the golden fields, it echoes so well.
A name so regal, a name so fine,
In every verse, it brightly shines.

Barbara, oh, Barbara, so full of grace,
In every heart, you find your place.
With a gentle touch and a kind embrace,
You bring joy to every space.

Barbara, like a blooming flower,
In every season, you exude power.
A name that dances on the wind,
And leaves a lasting, loving, splendid spin.

Barbara, a name that's a melody,
In every note, it sings with glee.
A name that paints the sky so blue,
And fills the world with warmth anew.

Barbara, a name so full of light,
In every darkness, you shine so bright.
A name that whispers tales untold,
And weaves dreams in every fold.
    Barbara, oh, Barbara, so pure and true,
In every moment, we cherish you.
A name that's like a precious gem,
And shines in every heart, a priceless emblem.

SIX

HERE'S TO YOU, BARBARA

Barbara, a name that glistens in the sun,
In every run, it shines for everyone.
A symphony of poise and grace,
In every space, it finds its place.

In the tapestry of life, your name unfolds,
A story of courage that's never been told.
With every syllable, a journey begins,
Of strength and kindness, it always wins.

Barbara, oh name that carries such might,
In every light, it's a guiding light.
A melody of love and resilience,
In every instance, it defies all silence.

With every letter, a new chapter takes flight,
Of dreams and triumphs, it reaches great height.

Barbara, a name that stands so tall,
In every call, it breaks down any wall.
    So here's to you, Barbara, so pure and true,
In every view, you light up the world anew.
With every rhyme, your name we acclaim,
A name that's never the same, a name that's our aim.

SEVEN

NAME SO DIVINE

Barbara, a name so elegant and rare,
Like a melody floating through the air,
In every syllable, a story to share,
In every letter, a beauty so fair.

Beneath the moonlit sky, Barbara dances,
Her spirit alive with endless romances,
A name that echoes in the heart's secret glances,
A name that in every language enhances.

Barbara, a name that holds ancient power,
A name that blooms like a wildflower,
In every verse, a name to empower,
In every moment, a name to devour.

In the whispers of the wind, Barbara's name sings,
A symphony of joy that forever clings,
In every note, a love that stings,
In every memory, a love that brings.

Barbara, a name that stands the test of time,
A name that sparkles like a rare find,
In every heartbeat, a name that chimes,
In every dream, a name that climbs.
So here's to Barbara, a name so divine,
In every thought, a name to enshrine,
In every poem, a name to intertwine,
In every soul, a name to define.

EIGHT

GUIDING LIGHT

Barbara, a name that shines like the morning sun,
A name that dances through fields, always on the run,
In every corner of the world, a name that's spun,
In every tale, a name that's never undone.

In the laughter of children, Barbara's name is heard,
A name that echoes like the song of a bird,
In every smile, a name that's never deterred,
In every adventure, a name that's always stirred.

Barbara, a name that holds a universe within,
A name that's like a rare and precious twin,
In every moment, a name that's a win,
In every journey, a name that's a colorful spin.

In the depths of the ocean, Barbara's name swims,
A name that glows like the evening's soft hymns,
In every wave, a name that never dims,
In every heartbeat, a name that brims.

So here's to Barbara, a name so bold and bright,
In every dream, a name that takes flight,
In every starry night, a name that feels just right,
In every memory, a name that's a guiding light.

NINE

NAME RESOUNDS

Barbara, a name that sparkles in the moon's embrace,
A name that paints the sky with grace,
In every echo, a name that finds its place,
In every moment, a name that leaves a trace.

In the whispers of the wind, Barbara's name weaves,
A tapestry of dreams that the heart believes,
In every whisper, a name that achieves,
In every bond, a name that cleaves.

Barbara, a name that blooms like a garden fair,
A name that dances with the scent of rare,
In every petal, a name that dares,
In every fragrance, a name that declares.

In the laughter of friends, Barbara's name resounds,
A symphony of joy that knows no bounds,

In every melody, a name that surrounds,
In every celebration, a name that rebounds.
    Barbara, a name that holds the stars in its gaze,
A name that travels through time's maze,
In every constellation, a name that plays,
In every universe, a name that stays.
    So here's to Barbara, a name so pure and true,
In every adventure, a name that's overdue,
In every sunrise, a name that's anew,
In every heart, a name that brews.

TEN

PROMISE OF TOMORROW

Barbara, a name that glows like the evening's first star,
A name that whispers secrets from afar,
In every tale, a name that leaves a scar,
In every journey, a name that's meant to spar.

In the colors of the sunset, Barbara's name ignites,
A symphony of hues that never fights,
In every stroke, a name that writes,
In every canvas, a name that excites.

Barbara, a name that blooms like a rare, exotic flower,
A name that waltzes through life's every hour,
In every petal, a name that empowers,
In every fragrance, a name that towers.

In the laughter of loved ones, Barbara's name sings,

A melody of love that forever clings,
In every note, a name that stings,
In every memory, a name that brings.

Barbara, a name that holds the promise of tomorrow,
A name that banishes all sorrow,
In every heartbeat, a name that's a gentle burrow,
In every dream, a name that's a fearless sparrow.

So here's to Barbara, a name so rare and divine,
In every thought, a name that's a lifeline,
In every whisper, a name that's a goldmine,
In every soul, a name that's a sacred shrine.

ELEVEN

DANCES IN THE MORNING LIGHT

Barbara, a name that dances in the morning light,
A name that paints the sky with colors bright,
In every sunrise, a name that takes flight,
In every dream, a name that feels just right.

In the embrace of nature, Barbara's name weaves,
A tapestry of beauty that the heart believes,
In every breeze, a name that never leaves,
In every season, a name that achieves.

Barbara, a name that blooms like a garden of delight,
A name that soothes like the stars at night,
In every whisper, a name that ignites,
In every moment, a name that invites.

In the laughter of friends, Barbara's name resounds,
A melody of joy that knows no bounds,

In every hug, a name that surrounds,
In every celebration, a name that astounds.
    Barbara, a name that holds the secrets of the earth,
A name that gives every soul a new birth,
In every heartbeat, a name that's a hearth,
In every memory, a name that's a worth.
    So here's to Barbara, a name so rare and true,
In every adventure, a name that's overdue,
In every sunrise, a name that's anew,
In every heart, a name that's forever in view.

TWELVE

PRECIOUS AND RARE

Barbara, a name that shimmers in the twilight glow,
A name that whispers secrets as the breezes blow,
In every echo, a name that casts a gentle show,
In every heartbeat, a name that lets love flow.

In the rhythm of nature, Barbara's name sings,
A melody that lifts the soul on gossamer wings,
In every verse, a name that embraces and clings,
In every symphony, a name that joyfully rings.

Barbara, a name that blooms like a rare and vibrant bloom,
A name that lights up even the darkest room,
In every petal, a name that banishes gloom,
In every fragrance, a name that dispels all fume.

In the laughter of loved ones, Barbara's name resonates,
A melody of warmth that eternally elevates,

In every smile, a name that jubilates,
In every embrace, a name that radiates.
 Barbara, a name that holds the dreams of many a soul,
A name that inspires and makes everyone whole,
In every wish, a name that plays a vital role,
In every heart, a name that makes life full.
 So here's to Barbara, a name so precious and rare,
In every journey, a name that's beyond compare,
In every sunrise, a name that's always there,
In every memory, a name that we gratefully declare.

THIRTEEN

DIAMOND IN THE SKY

Barbara, a name that sparkles like a diamond in the sky,
A name that whispers secrets with a gentle sigh,
In every moment, a name that never says goodbye,
In every dream, a name that reaches high.

In the silence of the night, Barbara's name glows,
A beacon of hope that the heart knows,
In every twinkle, a name that bestows,
In every wish, a name that forever grows.

Barbara, a name that blooms like a rare and precious rose,
A name that in every season, sweetly shows,
In every petal, a name that bestows,
In every fragrance, a name that peacefully flows.

In the laughter of friends, Barbara's name ignites,
A symphony of joy that forever delights,

In every smile, a name that unites,
In every celebration, a name that excites.
    Barbara, a name that holds the stories of the past,
A name that in every memory, eternally lasts,
In every heartbeat, a name that steadfastly casts,
In every journey, a name that universally broadcasts.
    So here's to Barbara, a name so cherished and true,
In every adventure, a name that stands anew,
In every sunrise, a name that beautifully imbues,
In every heart, a name that forever ensues.

FOURTEEN

HOPE AND LOVE

Barbara, a name so divine,
Like a melody, it does entwine,
In the hearts of those who hear,
A name that brings both joy and cheer.
In the garden, a Barbara rose,
Blooms with grace, its beauty shows,
A name of strength, a name of light,
Guiding through the darkest night.
Barbara, a name of history,
A tale of courage, a legacy,
From ancient times to modern days,
A name that shines in countless ways.
In art and music, Barbara's touch,
Inspires, enchants, and means so much,
A name that resonates with power,
In every passing, fleeting hour.

Barbara, a name that holds the key,
To unlock dreams and set them free,
A name that carries hope and love,
Guiding spirits from above.

So here's to Barbara, in all her glory,
A name that weaves a timeless story,
May her name forever soar and thrive,
In every heart where it's kept alive.

FIFTEEN

EVERY DREAM

Barbara, a name so rare and true,
Like a starlit sky, it shines on through,
In the tapestry of life it weaves,
A name that comforts, a name that relieves.

In the fields, a Barbara lily blooms,
Amidst the whispers and sweet perfumes,
A name of grace, a name of poise,
Embracing nature's gentle voice.

Barbara, a name of wisdom's light,
A beacon shining through the darkest night,
From ancient tales to modern lore,
A name that echoes forevermore.

In dance and theater, Barbara's grace,
Enchants the soul and leaves a trace,
A name that resonates with art,
A symphony that touches every heart.

Barbara, a name that stands so tall,
A fortress strong, yet tender to all,
A name that embodies love and care,
A melody that fills the air.

So here's to Barbara, in all her glory,
A name that writes a timeless story,
May her name forever brightly gleam,
In every moment, in every dream.

SIXTEEN

GLORY

Barbara, a name of elegance and grace,
A symphony of beauty in every trace,
In the tapestry of life, it holds its own,
A name that shines like a precious stone.

In the meadows, a Barbara daisy blooms,
Radiant and pure, banishing all glooms,
A name of resilience, a name of might,
Guiding through the darkness, bringing light.

Barbara, a name of stories untold,
Of bravery and warmth, a spirit bold,
From ancient legends to present-day,
A name that stands the test of time, they say.

In literature and verse, Barbara's song,
Echoes through the ages, steady and strong,
A name that sparks imagination's fire,
A muse for all who dare to aspire.

    Barbara, a name that resonates with love,
A gift from the heavens, ordained above,
A name that embodies compassion and care,
A beacon of hope, always there.
    So here's to Barbara, in all her glory,
A name that paints a wondrous story,
May her name forever brightly shine,
In every heart, in every line.

SEVENTEEN

SPUN GOLD

    Oh, Barbara, with hair like spun gold,
In your presence, stories unfold.
Your name, a melody sweet and bold,
In every heart, a tale untold.
    Barbara, the bearer of light,
In your eyes, the stars take flight.
A name that dances in the moon's soft glow,
And in the whispers of the winds that blow.
    Barbara, like a blooming rose,
In your grace, the garden grows.
With every step, a new path chose,
In your name, a symphony composed.
    Barbara, with a spirit so free,
In your laughter, the world finds glee.
A name that echoes through the hills and plains,
And in the rhythm of the gentle rains.

Barbara, like a shimmering stream,
In your presence, dreams gleam.
With every heartbeat, a new verse to sing,
In your name, a vibrant offering.

Barbara, a name that holds such power,
In your essence, a timeless flower.
A name that paints the sky with hues so grand,
And in every whisper of the grains of sand.

Barbara, a name to cherish and adore,
In your name, a symphony to explore.
A name that resonates through time and space,
And in every heart, a sacred place.

EIGHTEEN

RIVERS THAT FLOW

Oh, Barbara, like a beacon in the night,
With your name, the world feels so bright.
In every smile, a spark ignites,
In your presence, the soul takes flight.
 Barbara, a name that sings with grace,
In your aura, a wondrous embrace.
A name that weaves through the tapestry of time,
And in every moment, a new paradigm.
 Barbara, like a melody so pure,
In your name, the heart finds its cure.
With every breath, a new story unfurls,
In your essence, a symphony whirls.
 Barbara, a name that blooms like a flower,
In your gaze, the world finds its power.
A name that dances in the sun's warm glow,
And in the whispers of the rivers that flow.

Barbara, with a spirit so free,
In your laughter, the world finds glee.
A name that echoes through the mountains and plains,
And in the rhythm of the gentle rains.

Barbara, like a star in the night,
In your name, the universe feels so right.
With every step, a new journey begins,
In your name, a timeless melody spins.

Barbara, a name that holds such might,
In your presence, the world feels so right.
A name that paints the sky with hues so grand,
And in every whisper of the grains of sand.

Barbara, a name to cherish and adore,
In your name, a symphony to explore.
A name that resonates through time and space,
And in every heart, a sacred place.

NINETEEN

ECHOES THROUGH THE AGES

Barbara, a name that echoes through the ages,
In your presence, the world turns its pages.
A name that dances in the moon's soft glow,
And in the whispers of the winds that blow.

Oh, Barbara, with eyes like the morning dew,
In your name, the sky feels so new.
In every smile, a story takes flight,
In your essence, a symphony of light.

Barbara, like a gentle breeze in the spring,
In your laughter, the heart finds its wings.
A name that weaves through the tapestry of time,
And in every moment, a new paradigm.

Barbara, a name that glistens like the sea,
In your aura, the soul feels so free.

With every step, a new path unfolds,
In your name, a story yet untold.
    Barbara, a name that blooms like a rose,
In your grace, the garden of life grows.
A name that paints the sky with hues so grand,
And in every whisper of the grains of sand.
    Barbara, like a melody in the night,
In your presence, the world feels so right.
A name that resonates through time and space,
And in every heart, a sacred place.
    Barbara, a name that holds such power,
In your essence, a timeless flower.
A name that echoes through the hills and plains,
And in the rhythm of the gentle rains.
    Barbara, a name to cherish and adore,
In your name, a symphony to explore.
A name that sings with grace and might,
In your presence, the world feels so bright.

TWENTY

EVERY PRAYER

Barbara, oh sweet name of grace,
In every letter, a story to embrace.
Beneath the stars, your name takes flight,
A melody of beauty, shining bright.
Bountiful as the ocean's waves,
A name that echoes through the caves.
Barbara, a symphony of sound,
In every whisper, love is found.
In gardens blooming with fragrant blooms,
Barbara, your name forever looms.
A tapestry of colors, woven with care,
A name that dances in the air.
In the realm of dreams, your name abides,
Where fantasies and reality coincide.
Barbara, a name of endless charm,
In every corner, it does no harm.

In the gallery of life, your name's on display,
A masterpiece that will never sway.
Barbara, a name that stands the test of time,
In every verse, a rhythm so sublime.

So let's raise a toast to Barbara's name,
A beacon of hope in a world so tame.
In every heartbeat, in every prayer,
Barbara, a name beyond compare.

TWENTY-ONE

UNYIELDING POWER

Barbara, a name that dances in the breeze,
Whispered by the ancient trees.
In every sunrise, in every dawn,
A name that lingers, never withdrawn.

In the tapestry of time, Barbara shines,
A name that echoes through the vines.
In the symphony of life, a melodious hum,
Barbara, a name that leaves us numb.

Beneath the moon's enchanting glow,
Barbara's name continues to grow.
In every meadow, in every glade,
A name that never seems to fade.

Barbara, a name that weaves through dreams,
In every echo, a thousand streams.
In the labyrinth of thoughts, it finds a way,
A name that brightens the darkest day.

In the garden of hope, Barbara blooms,
Dispelling darkness, lifting glooms.
A name that paints the sky with hues,
In every heart, a name that ensues.

So let's raise our voices to Barbara's name,
A beacon of light, a burning flame.
In every moment, in every hour,
Barbara, a name of unyielding power.

TWENTY-TWO

DANCES IN THE AIR

Barbara, a name like a symphony,
Resonating through history.
In every whisper, in every song,
A name that's been cherished all along.

In the tapestry of time, Barbara weaves,
Through every heart, it gently cleaves.
In the dance of light, in the shadow's play,
Barbara's name glimmers, come what may.

In the garden of words, Barbara blooms,
A name that dispels all worldly glooms.
In every smile, in every tear,
Barbara's name echoes, crystal clear.

Barbara, a name that paints the sky,
With hues of courage, soaring high.
In the labyrinth of dreams, it takes flight,
A name that conquers the darkest night.

In the whispers of the wind, Barbara's name is heard,
A melody that can't be deterred.
In every echo, in every sigh,
Barbara's name soars, reaching high.

So let's celebrate Barbara's name today,
A timeless treasure, come what may.
In every heartbeat, in every prayer,
Barbara's name dances in the air.

TWENTY-THREE

WONDROUS SPACE

Barbara, oh how your name sings,
Like a melody that forever rings,
In the hearts of those who know,
The beauty of your name's sweet flow.

Barbara, with each letter so fine,
Like stars in the midnight sky, they shine,
A name that holds such grace and might,
Guiding us through the darkest night.

In every syllable, a story untold,
Of courage, wisdom, and love's stronghold,
Barbara, a name that stands so tall,
In the symphony of names, the grandest of all.

Like a garden in full bloom,
Barbara, your name dispels all gloom,
A beacon of hope, a guiding light,
Guiding us through the darkest night.

In every consonant and every vowel,
Lies a world of strength and a heart so foul,
Barbara, your name is a work of art,
A masterpiece that sets us apart.

So here's to you, our dear Barbara fair,
A name so rare, beyond compare,
May it always be spoken with love and grace,
In every corner of this wondrous space.

TWENTY-FOUR

LOVE AND CHEER

Barbara, a name that dances on the air,
A symphony of sounds so sweet and rare,
In every letter, a tale is spun,
Of triumph, grace, and battles won.

Barbara, like a gentle breeze,
Whispering secrets through the trees,
A name that carries strength and light,
Guiding us through the darkest night.

In each syllable, a world unfolds,
Of courage, kindness, and stories untold,
Barbara, a name so bold and true,
A beacon of hope in all that we do.

Like a tapestry woven with care,
Barbara, your name is beyond compare,
A masterpiece of love and grace,
In every corner of this wondrous space.

In every consonant, a promise made,
Of loyalty, honor, and never to fade,
Barbara, your name shines so bright,
A guiding star in the darkest night.

So here's to you, our dear Barbara divine,
A name that will forever shine,
May it always be spoken with love and cheer,
For in the name Barbara, there's magic here.

TWENTY-FIVE

FAIR AND SWEET

Barbara, oh name so fair and sweet,
In your presence, hearts skip a beat.
With grace and charm, you light up the day,
In every possible and imaginable way.

Your name, a melody that rings so true,
A symphony of beauty, through and through.
Barbara, like a rare and precious gem,
A name that shines, a priceless diadem.

In gardens of words, your name blooms bright,
A floral tapestry, a wondrous sight.
Barbara, a name that dances on the breeze,
A lullaby whispered through rustling trees.

In the realm of names, you reign supreme,
A regal presence, a delightful dream.
Barbara, a name that sparkles like the stars,
A constellation of wonder, beyond all memoirs.

In every language, your name holds sway,
A universal anthem, come what may.
Barbara, a name that paints the sky with love,
A masterpiece crafted from the heavens above.
Oh, Barbara, your name we celebrate,
In every verse, your charm we elevate.
A name so unique, a treasure to behold,
In every story and legend, your name is told.

TWENTY-SIX

EVERLASTING MYSTERY

Barbara, your impact knows no bounds,
In hearts and minds, your name resounds.
With kindness and warmth, you touch each soul,
Leaving a legacy that's beyond all control.

Your name, a beacon in the darkest night,
Guiding lost souls towards the light.
Barbara, a name that ignites a fire within,
Inspiring greatness, helping others to win.

In every tale of triumph and glory,
Your name weaves into each character's story.
Barbara, a name that brings out the best,
A catalyst for change, a force to manifest.

In the tapestry of lives, your name weaves through,
A thread of hope, a love so true.

Barbara, a name that etches itself in history,
A legacy of love, an everlasting mystery.

TWENTY-SEVEN

RARE FLOWER

Barbara, a name that sings with grace,
In every syllable, a wondrous trace.
Like a gentle breeze on a summer's day,
Your name dances with joy in every way.

With strength and wisdom, your name is crowned,
In every challenge, your spirit is found.
Barbara, a name that echoes through time,
A melody of resilience, a rhythm so sublime.

In the gallery of names, yours is a masterpiece,
A work of art that will never cease.
Barbara, a name that blooms like a rare flower,
A symbol of elegance, a symbol of power.

In the symphony of life, your name takes the lead,
A harmonious tune that everyone needs.
Barbara, a name that paints the world with love,
A portrait of compassion, a blessing from above.

In the tapestry of friendships, your name weaves strong,
A bond that lasts, an eternal song.
Barbara, a name that lights up the darkest night,
A beacon of hope, a comforting sight.
Oh, Barbara, your name we cherish dear,
In every whisper, in every cheer.
A name so unique, a treasure to hold,
In every story and legend, your name is told.

TWENTY-EIGHT

RESONATES

Barbara, a name that sparkles like the dew,
In every sunrise, in every view.
With elegance and poise, you light up the scene,
A radiant presence, serene and keen.

Your name, a melody that soothes the soul,
A symphony of kindness, making others whole.
Barbara, like a rare and precious pearl,
A name that shines, in every swirl.

In the tapestry of names, yours stands tall,
A beacon of hope, for one and all.
Barbara, a name that resonates with care,
A sanctuary of love, beyond compare.

In the garden of dreams, your name blossoms bright,
A floral symphony, a mesmerizing sight.

Barbara, a name that dances with the stars,
A celestial waltz, beyond earthly bars.
    In the novel of life, your name writes a tale,
A narrative of compassion, that will never pale.
Barbara, a name that etches itself in hearts,
A masterpiece of empathy, as each storyline starts.
    Oh, Barbara, your name we celebrate,
In every stanza, your aura we appreciate.
A name so unique, a treasure to behold,
In every memory and chronicle, your name is extolled.

TWENTY-NINE

TREASURE TO EMBRACE

Barbara, a name that glows with grace,
Like a sunbeam's kiss on a tranquil place.
In every step, a dance of elegance and charm,
A symphony of virtues, a soothing balm.

Your name, a tapestry of colors so bright,
A masterpiece of joy, a radiant light.
Barbara, like a rare and precious gem,
A name that shimmers, a celestial hymn.

In the mosaic of names, yours stands tall,
A beacon of strength, for one and all.
Barbara, a name that whispers tales of love,
A sanctuary of kindness, soaring above.

In the garden of aspirations, your name blooms fair,
A floral sonnet, a vision beyond compare.

Barbara, a name that resonates with care,
A haven of compassion, beyond compare.
 In the novel of existence, your name scribes a story,
A narrative of resilience, in all its glory.
Barbara, a name that etches itself in hearts,
A masterpiece of empathy, as each storyline starts.
 Oh, Barbara, your name we hold in esteem,
In every ballad, your essence gleams.
A name so unique, a treasure to embrace,
In every fable and legend, your name finds its place.

THIRTY

BEYOND ANY DREAM

Barbara, oh name so fair,
With elegance beyond compare,
In the garden of names, you're the rarest flower,
A name that holds an enchanting power.
  Your syllables dance like a melody,
A name that's timeless, oh so lovely,
In every letter, a story unfolds,
A name that's cherished, a sight to behold.
  Barbara, a gem among the rest,
A name that stands out, simply the best,
In the tapestry of names, you shine bright,
A name that brings warmth and light.
  From B to A, R to A, each letter sings,
A name that echoes through the valleys and springs,
In every language, your beauty is known,
A name that's regal, a name to be shown.

Barbara, a name that commands grace,
A name that time cannot erase,
In every heart, your presence is felt,
A name that makes the universe melt.
So here's to Barbara, a name so divine,
A name that's rare, like a sparkling wine,
In every poem, your essence will gleam,
Barbara, a name beyond any dream.

THIRTY-ONE

ILLUSTRIOUS LEGACY

Barbara, a name like a gentle whisper in the wind,
A name that carries a mystical and enchanting spin,
In the grand tapestry of names, you stand tall and resplendent,
A name that resonates through it all, ever transcendent.

From the 'B' that begins your name's wondrous tale,
To the 'A' that follows with a graceful and elegant trail,
Barbara, a name that's a captivating work of art,
A name that enthralls and captivates every heart.

In every syllable, a rich and vibrant story is masterfully weaved,
A name that's cherished, beloved, and deeply believed,
From the 'R' that rolls off the tongue with a melodic hum,

To the 'A' that lingers, ever so youthful and yet so calmly numb.

Barbara, a name that's a melodious and harmonious symphony,
A name that paints a vivid and lively artistic tapestry,
In every corner of the world, your name glows and shines,
A name that blooms and flourishes like a radiant and timeless vine.

With each letter, a grand and illustrious legacy is carved,
A name that's timeless, forever starved and yet so carved,
For more recognition, more admiration, more loving veneration,
Barbara, a name that sparks fascination and profound admiration.

So here's to Barbara, a name so divine and utterly refined,
A name that outshines, like a rare and exquisite vintage wine,
In every verse, your name will gleam and radiantly beam,
Barbara, a name that's beyond any dream, a name that's a poet's cherished theme.

THIRTY-TWO

WORK OF ART

Oh, Barbara, thy name doth ring with grace,
A melody that time cannot erase.
In gardens fair, where blooms the sweetest rose,
Thy name is whispered, where love forever flows.
 Barbara, like the stars that brightly shine,
A beacon of hope, a love so divine.
In fields of gold, where dreams take flight,
Thy name is spoken with pure delight.
 Oh, Barbara, in the tapestry of life,
Thy name weaves through joy and strife.
With every syllable, a tale is told,
Of courage, kindness, and hearts so bold.
 Barbara, in the whispers of the wind,
A name that carries the power to mend.
In the dance of life, a rhythm so pure,
Thy name is a symphony, an eternal allure.

Oh, Barbara, in the symphony of words,
Thy name is sung by the chirping birds.
In every verse, in every line,
Thy name shines bright, a treasure so fine.

Barbara, in the echoes of time,
A name that eternally will shine.
In every heart, in every prayer,
Thy name will linger, beyond compare.

Barbara, a name so rich and rare,
A tapestry of beauty beyond compare.
In every soul, in every heart,
Thy name will forever be a work of art.

THIRTY-THREE

RAISE A TOAST

Barbara, a name so grand and true,
In the vast ocean of names, it shines through,
Like a beacon of strength and grace,
A name that time cannot erase.

In the gardens of language, it blooms,
A symphony of letters, dispelling gloom,
Barbara, a melody on the lips of many,
A name that echoes through history.

In the tapestry of life, it weaves,
A name that empowers and believes,
In each syllable, a story untold,
Of resilience and courage, manifold.

Barbara, a name that stands tall,
In the face of adversity, it never falls,
A name of wisdom, of love, of light,
Guiding hearts through the darkest night.

In the dictionary of dreams, it's defined,
As a name of beauty, of a rare kind,
Barbara, a name that's here to stay,
In every heart, in every word, in every way.
So let's raise a toast to Barbara's name,
A symphony of letters, an eternal flame,
In this world of names, it's a shining star,
Barbara, a name that's truly bizarre.

THIRTY-FOUR

YOUR NAME

Barbara, a name that dances with delight,
In every note, in every starry night.
With grace and poise, you paint the sky,
A symphony of wonder, soaring high.

Your name, a melody that echoes true,
A serenade of beauty, in all you do.
Barbara, like a rare and precious treasure,
A name that glimmers, a joy without measure.

In the gallery of names, yours stands strong,
A lighthouse of hope, a comforting song.
Barbara, a name that resonates with love,
A sanctuary of kindness, high above.

In the garden of dreams, your name blooms bright,
A floral tapestry, a captivating sight.
Barbara, a name that sparkles like the dawn,
A radiant aura, from dusk till morn.

In the novel of life, your name weaves a tale,
A narrative of compassion, never frail.
Barbara, a name that etches itself in hearts,
A masterpiece of empathy, as each story starts.

Oh, Barbara, your name we celebrate,
In every verse, your spirit elevates.
A name so unique, a treasure to behold,
In every memory and legend, your name is told.

ABOUT THE AUTHOR

Walter the Educator is one of the pseudonyms for Walter Anderson. Formally educated in Chemistry, Business, and Education, he is an educator, an author, a diverse entrepreneur, and he is the son of a disabled war veteran. "Walter the Educator" shares his time between educating and creating. He holds interests and owns several creative projects that entertain, enlighten, enhance, and educate, hoping to inspire and motivate you.

Follow, find new works, and stay up to date
with Walter the Educator™
at WaltertheEducator.com

www.ingramcontent.com/pod-product-compliance
Lightning Source LLC
LaVergne TN
LVHW010604070526
838199LV00063BA/5070